PROJECTS ABOUT

The Ancient Aztecs

David C. King

Marshall Cavendish Benchmark

New York

Acknowledgments

Many thanks to Sharon Flitterman-King for her expertise, especially with the activities.

Benchmark Books
Marshall Cavendish
99 White Plains Road
Tarrytown, NY 10591-9001
www.marshallcavendish.us

Text Copyright © 2006 by Marshall Cavendish Corporation
Illustrations and map Copyright © 2006 by Marshall Cavendish Corporation

Library of Congress Cataloging-in-Publication Data

King, David C.
Projects about the ancient Aztecs / by David C. King.
     p. cm.—(Hands-on history)
Summary: "Includes social studies projects taken from the ancient Aztecs"—Provided by publisher.
Includes bibliographical references and index.
ISBN-13: 978-0-7614-2256-3
ISBN-10: 0-7614-2256-0
1. Handicraft—Mexico—Juvenile literature. 2. Aztecs—Social life and customs—Juvenile literature. 3. Mexico—History—To 1519—Juvenile literature. I. Title. II. Series.
TT28.K56 2006
972'.01—dc22
                2006002812

Title page: A reconstruction of an Aztec calendar.
Illustrations by Rodica Prato
Map by XNR Productions
Photo Research by Joan Meisel

Photo credits: *Art Resource*, NY: 8, *Nick Saunders/Barbara Heller Photo Library*, London; 33, Werner Forman; *Corbis*: 1, 21, Gianni Dagli Orti; 4, *Free Agents Limited*; 12, Keith Dannemiller; 25, 28, Werner Forman; 32, *Bettmann*; *North Wind Picture Archives*: 7, 18, 34

Printed in China

1 3 5 6 4 2

Contents

❧

The Pyramid of the Sun is the third largest pyramid in the world at about 200 feet high by 700 feet wide.

1
Introduction

The Aztecs were worshippers of a sun god. And like the sun, their empire blazed across the pages of history—but only for a short time. Between 1300 and 1520 CE they came to rule over much of the land that is now Mexico. Through conquest and trade they controlled more than five hundred other tribal societies and ruled nearly six million people.

This book will carry you back in time six hundred years to the glory days of the mighty Aztec Empire. You'll discover that while they were feared warriors, the real foundation of their civilization was agriculture. Their farming techniques enabled them to produce an abundance of food. This meant that many people, instead of farming, could develop the special skills needed to build magnificent cities and create beautiful craft items and works of art. Their capital city, Tenochtitlán, built on an island in Lake Texcoco, was the largest and most spectacular city in the world at that time.

In your time travel to Tenochtitlán, you can try your hand at Aztec crafts, including weaving, using natural dyes, and making a tin rooster. You can also try writing Aztec pictographs and creating a folding book called a **codex**. You'll also make two of the foods that originated in the Americas: tortillas and hot chocolate.

The Aztec Empire ended as suddenly as it had appeared. In 1517 a Spanish soldier, or **conquistador**, named Hernán Cortés led a small army against the Aztecs. The conquerors destroyed Tenochtitlán and absorbed the Aztecs into the empire of New Spain. By 1520 the Aztec Empire was gone.

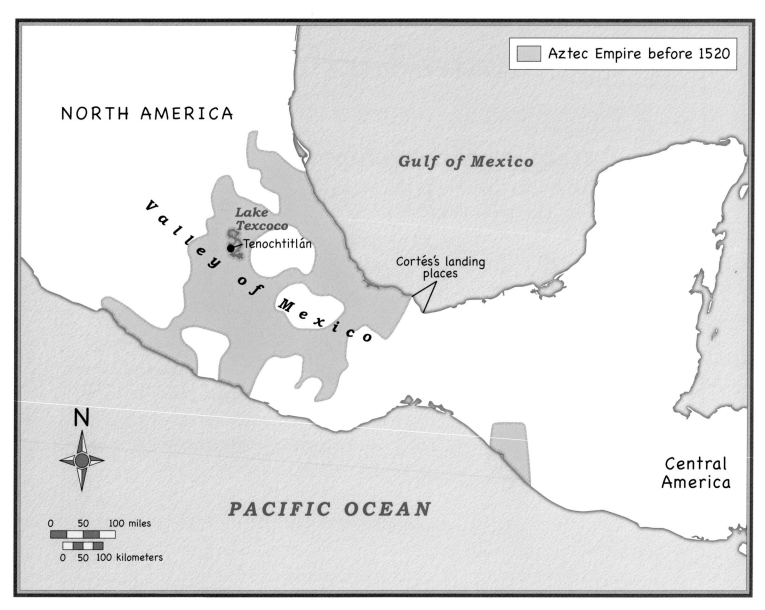

The Aztec Empire was located in the Valley of Mexico, and the site of Tenochtitlán is located under present-day Mexico City. The valley is unusual because it is located on a large plateau, so that the floor of the valley is actually at eight thousand feet. That's more than a mile above sea level.

The Spanish army had crossbows and armored horses to defeat the Aztecs, who used lances and swords.

The remains of the *chinampas* or floating gardens as they look today.

2

The Land of Plenty

The Aztecs made use of a variety of farming techniques to improve agricultural production. Crops were rotated, for example, which kept the soil from wearing out. And although the climate was dry, a series of small, shallow lakes held plenty of water. The Aztecs tapped into that supply by building irrigation canals to spread the water to the farm fields.

One of their great achievements was a system of **chinampas**. These are often called floating gardens because that's what they look like—rectangular garden plots set in the middle of a lake. *Chinampas* were made by building up layers of mud and sediment from the swampy bottom of the lake. Willows were planted around the edges, and tree roots held the soil in place. Channels of open water between the *chinampas* became water highways for the farmers' canoes.

Only about half the land in this broad valley was suitable for farming. The rest was too hilly or was covered by a chain of small, shallow lakes. Through the creative use of irrigation, crop rotation, and other techniques, such as reclaiming swampland, the Aztecs were able to grow an abundance of food. They had a large enough surplus of some crops, such as corn, that they could trade for farm products that did not do well in their valley, such as cotton and tropical fruits.

Food Gifts to the World

When Europeans first came to the Americas following the voyages of Christopher Columbus (1492-1503), they were surprised to learn of foods that were unknown in other parts of the world. In fact, about half the foods eaten in the world today originated in North and South America. Many of these Native American foods were grown in the lands of the Aztec Empire, including corn, sweet potatoes, squashes, pumpkins, beans, avocados, peanuts, vanilla, chocolate, chili peppers, and pineapples.

Tortillas

Your mother cooks not only for your family but also for the royal palace of the great Montezuma. She is one of many who give their time to preparing food for the palace, where nearly two thousand people live. It is 1509, and you are now finally old enough to help your mother make tortillas.

"How many tortillas do we have to make?" you ask.

"Well, the palace will need about ten thousand tortillas today," your mother answers. "Don't worry. We don't have to make them all. But maybe later you can help prepare the three hundred pounds of beans the steward has requested."

You will need:

- 2 cups flour or cornmeal
- 1 teaspoon baking powder
- 1 teaspoon salt
- 1 tablespoon butter or margarine
- cooking oil or spray
- 5 ounces cold tap water
- mixing bowl

- mixing spoon
- rolling pin
- frying pan or pancake griddle
- pancake flipper
- adult helper

Makes 12 tortillas

1. First, wash your hands. Then, in a mixing bowl, stir together the flour, baking powder, and salt. Rub in the butter or margarine until the mixture looks like breadcrumbs.

2. Add the water, and mix with your hands into a dough.

3. Form the dough into twelve balls. Sprinkle a little flour on a clean countertop, and roll out each ball into a flat pancake.

4. Have an adult help you coat a frying pan with a little cooking oil and fry the tortillas very quickly.

5. Serve your tortillas with butter and fold them around any kind of filling you like.

Cacao pods are opened and their seeds are removed in the process of making chocolate.

Hot Chocolate

It is the year 1535. Your father has just returned home to Madrid, Spain, after serving four years as governor of a province in New Spain. New Spain is the name given to the new Spanish Empire that covers much of the Valley of Mexico and large parts of South America.

As a treat, he prepares a new drink he learned of from the Aztecs in New Spain. "The native people use the bean of the cacao plant," he explains. "They make something called chocolate. It's very bitter, but by adding honey, it becomes quite tasty. I've made a hot drink for you to try."

You will need:

- 1 cup boiling water
- ¼ cup cocoa
- ⅛ teaspoon salt
- 2 to 4 tablespoons sugar
- ½ teaspoon cinnamon
- 3 cups milk

- double boiler
- saucepan
- whisk
- adult helper

Makes 4 servings

1. Combine the water, cocoa, salt, and sugar in the top of a double boiler. Remember to have an adult with you when you're using the stove.

2. Bring the water in the bottom of the double boiler to a boil, then reduce the heat to low. As the mixture becomes warm add the cinnamon.

3. Scald the milk in a small saucepan—that is, bring it quickly just to a boil. Then add it to the top of the double boiler. Cover, and keep the mixture over hot water for another 10 minutes.

4. Beat with a wire whisk until it's frothy. Serve hot.

Aztec Calendar Stone

The year is 1485. As the child of a palace steward, you are learning to use the Aztec calendar. There are really two calendars. One divides the year into 365 days. This helps farmworkers know exactly when to plant each crop. If they are wrong, an entire growing season could be lost. The other calendar divides the year into 260 days. Priests keep track of this calendar for planning religious ceremonies and festivals.

Your father needs to keep track of both calendars, using one to give directions to farm families and the other to plan palace events. To help you learn how to use the calendars, he helps you make a model out of potter's clay. The model is based on the huge calendar stone in the Great Temple. That stone measures twelve feet in diameter and weighs twenty-four tons. You'll make your calendar stone out of salt dough. Painted bright colors, it will make an unusual and attractive decoration.

You will need:

A. For salt dough
- 3 cups flour (not self-rising)
- 1 ¼ cups warm tap water
- 1 cup salt
- mixing bowl and spoon

1. Pour 1 cup of salt into the bowl and add the tap water, stirring steadily until the salt is dissolved.

2. Slowly stir in the flour, then mix with your hands until the salt dough is formed. Keep shaping it until it's smooth and firm. Form it into a ball.

3. If you need to store it, wrap it in wax paper and refrigerate. It will keep for up to a week.

You will need:

B. For the calendar stone

- salt dough
- scrap of paper and pencil
- round object to form circle (about 3 ¾ inches in diameter)
- rolling pin
- cutting board

- cookie sheet
- plastic knife, craft stick, toothpicks
- tempera paints: red, blue, yellow, gold
- paintbrushes
- acrylic varnish
- adult helper

1. On a piece of scrap paper, draw a design for your calendar stone: copy the design shown on page 17, or make your own. For example, you might divide the circle into twelve months or into fifty-two weeks.

2. Preheat the oven to 250° F.

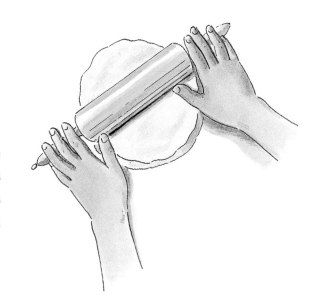

3. With a rolling pin, roll out a piece of the dough large enough to make a circle 3 ¾ inches in diameter and about ½ inch thick. Use a glass or other round object to press into the dough to make the circle.

4. Move the circle onto a cookie sheet. Use pieces of dough to shape features, such as sun rays, eyes, mouth, ears, tongue. Attach pieces by pressing them into the dough. Wet your fingers and smooth over the seams. Use a craft stick or plastic knife to make shapes. Make a small hole at the top for hanging. (Why is the tongue sticking out? This is probably because of the Aztec practice of bloodletting. Religious events were celebrated by a priest drawing blood, usually from his tongue.)

5. Bake for about 50 minutes or until the salt dough is golden brown. Allow it to cool.

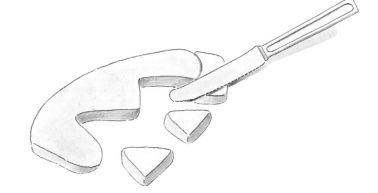

6. When cool, paint your calendar stone with bright tempera colors. When the paint is dry, spray the stone with acrylic varnish to preserve it.

A neighborhood of stone in the Aztec city of Tenochtitlán.

3

The Island City

When Spanish soldiers and priests first saw the Aztec city of Tenochtitlán, they could hardly believe its size and splendor. The city was originally built on two small islands in Lake Texcoco, but it spread onto *chinampas* and to suburblike settlements on the shore. The city and surrounding settlements held a population estimated at 400,000 people, far larger than any city in Europe. A Spanish explorer described seeing "great towers and temples rising from the water and all built of stone." The scene was so amazing, he said, that "some of our soldiers asked whether the things we saw were but a dream."

Most of the people in Tenochtitlán had nonfarming occupations. The largest number were craftworkers, including potters, jewelry makers, featherworkers, goldsmiths, silversmiths, and others. Families skilled in each craft formed guilds, like unions, and usually lived in the same neighborhoods. Other city dwellers included priests, government officials, merchants, and traders. The merchants and traders arranged open markets where people could trade for items brought from distant lands, including gold, precious stones, animal skins, and exotic birds.

Pictograms

Your fifteen-year-old brother is in his first year at the *telpuchcalli*, a school that includes military training. He also studies subjects like history and astronomy. "But the hardest of all," he says, "is writing."

The Aztecs used a system of picture writing. The pictures, or **glyphs**, were **pictograms**. Some pictograms were pictures of objects, such as a rabbit, knife, tree, or house. Other glyphs were **ideographs**, pictures that described ideas. Footprints would mean travel, for example, and a shield and club represented war.

"I would like to be a scribe," your brother explains. "It is an honored profession. But," he adds with a grin, "first I have to learn to read and draw!"

Aztec writing appeared not only in books but also on vases, walls, and other objects. You can use your pictograms to decorate an unpainted paper or plastic bowl or plate, or unpainted pottery (available at craft stores).

Aztec scribes and painters focused on different tasks. Some marked births and deaths; others recorded business deals, historical events, or kept law books.

You will need:

- several sheets of newspaper
- unpainted pottery, or paper or plastic bowl or plate
- pencil and scrap paper

- felt-tip pen, black, fine point
- tempera paints or acrylics: red, blue, yellow
- small brush

1. Spread several sheets of newspaper on your work surface.

2. Use pencil and scrap paper to practice drawing some of the glyphs shown here (or invent your own).

3. Copy some of the pictograms onto your unpainted bowl or plate. You can use pencil to make the drawing, but then darken the outline with a felt-tip pen. Make the drawing large enough so that you can paint it.

4. Paint your pictograms with bright colors. Use your finished object for decoration rather than for food.

Codex

The year is 1496. At a huge market in Tenochtitlán, you stop to watch an elderly scribe writing a codex, an Aztec book. He sits on the ground, cross-legged, with his brushes, paints, and the codex on a low table. Other **codices** are in bundles next to him.

"I am recording some rules of behavior," the scribe explains. He reads some of them to you:

"Do not spill food on another person's clothing."

"Do not eat fast or smack your lips as you chew."

"Always be kind to the sick, the elderly, and the disabled."

A scribe was called a *tlacuilo,* "book artist," and books or codices were called thought paintings. Codices were made on long strips of deerskin or bark paper, about eight inches wide. A codex could be twenty feet long or longer. It was folded like an accordion into smaller panels.

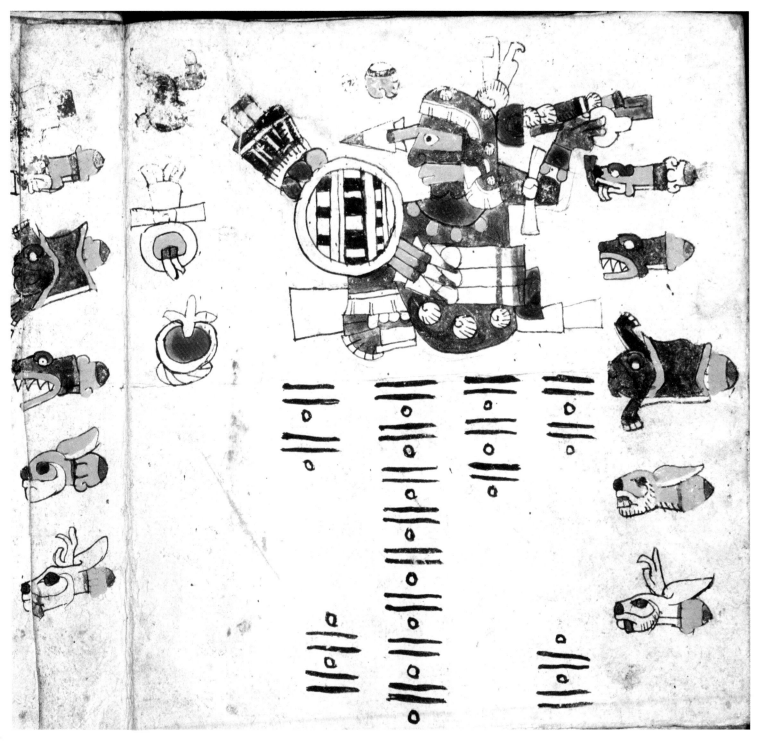

Detail of a codex. Most were destroyed by Spanish conquistadors.

You will need:

- two sheets of white paper, 8 ½ by 11 inches
- scissors
- two pieces of poster board, each 5 inches by 6 inches, white or any color
- transparent tape
- white glue
- pencil
- felt-tip pen, black, fine or medium point
- colored pencils or crayons

1. Fold both sheets of paper in half the long way. Cut each piece in half at the fold, creating four long, narrow sheets.

2. Fold each of these long sheets in half the short way. Overlap the edges and attach them with transparent tape, as shown in the drawing. Crease the fold at each edge to make an accordion-style book.

3. Use the pieces of poster board to make a front and back cover, gluing the covers to the end sheets.

4. Use your book for writing poems, ideas, or a story. Or use it to collect pictures, pressed flowers, or drawings of Aztec pictograms. Decorate the front cover with your name.

Ceremonial Mask

On the steps of a temple in Tenochtitlán a woman is working on a mask for next week's festival of the flowers. The mask is made with pieces of **turquoise** and **obsidian.** "I'll also use some bits of seashell for the face," she explains, showing you a tray of colorful shells. "Would you like to pick out two shells for the eyes?" she asks.

Festivals with music and dancing were almost daily events. Music was supplied by drums and a variety of flutelike instruments. Most ceremonies had a religious connection. Two of the most important gods were **Quetzalcoatl**, called "the Feathered Serpent," who was responsible for human life, and **Huitzilopochtli**, or "the Hummingbird of the Left," who was the Aztec warrior god.

You can use your Aztec ceremonial mask as an unusual and colorful wall hanging.

You will need:

- measuring cup
- several sheets of newspaper
- flour
- 3 cups water, plus 1 cup cold water
- teakettle
- newspaper or paper towels
- medium-sized saucepan
- mixing spoon
- ruler
- petroleum jelly
- disposable aluminum pie plate, about 9 inches in diameter
- large nail
- string
- poster paint, any colors
- small paintbrush
- adult helper

An Aztec turquoise mask.

1. Ask an adult to help you heat about 3 cups of water in a teakettle. Bring it to a gentle boil.

2. While the water is heating, measure the flour into the saucepan. Slowly stir in 1 cup of cold tap water. Keep on stirring until you have a smooth paste with no lumps.

3. Ask the adult to slowly stir in about 1 ½ cups of the hot water. Continue stirring until smooth. If the paste feels too thick, stir in more hot water.

4. Cook the mixture over medium heat for 2 or 3 minutes, stirring occasionally. Turn off the heat and let the mixture cool for about 15 minutes.

5. While the mixture is cooling, tear forty or fifty strips of paper, each 4 to 6 inches long and 1 inch wide. (It's easier to tear if you tear the paper along the edge of a ruler.)

6. Spread several sheets of newspaper on your work surface. Place the pie tin upside down on the newspaper, and cover the tin completely with a thin coating of petroleum jelly. This will prevent the papier-mâché from sticking.

7. Dip a strip of paper into the paste, covering it completely; then pull it between your fingers to remove the excess paste.

8. Apply the pasted paper to the pie tin. Continue applying pasted strips, overlapping them and smoothing them down to remove any bubbles. After the tin is completely covered, add a second layer, placing the strips in a different direction, making a crisscross pattern.

9. Add two or three more layers, each time in the crisscross pattern.

10. Remove the leftover paste from the saucepan. If it has started to harden, add a little water.

11. Allow the papier-mâché to dry completely for about five days before you remove it from the pie tin. If it sticks, gently pry it off with a table knife.

12. Paint your mask with bright colors, adding eyes, nose, and mouth. For a second coat, wait about one hour for the first coat to dry. Paint hair on your mask or apply strips of yarn. Work a nail through either side of the mask, about one-third of the way from the top. Tie a string on the back of the mask from one side to the other.

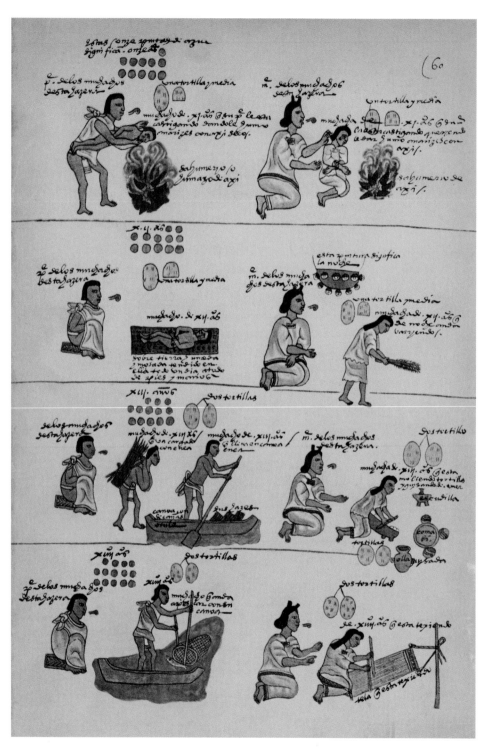

This ancient manuscript shows Aztecs doing a variety of daily tasks.

4

The Aztec Way of Life

About half the people in the Aztec Empire made their living by farming. Their advanced methods enabled farm families to provide abundant food, not only for themselves but also for the thousands of city dwellers. The city population was made up of craftworkers, merchants, priests, government officials, and soldiers.

The families of craftworkers formed guilds that established rules to protect the craft from shoddy work or charging high prices. Guild families lived in the same neighborhood and trained their sons and daughters in the craft. Crafts included stone carving, weaving, pottery, goldsmithing, metalworking, and featherworking.

Smooth Aztec pottery was made for the tables of nobles and priests. Everyday pottery had a rough surface, making it easier to handle.

Farmworkers joined city people for religious celebrations held at pyramid-shaped temples. The Aztecs believed that their major gods required human sacrifice to restore their strength in their struggle against the forces of darkness. Standing at the top of the pyramid steps, priests presided over the sacrificial killing. The victims were usually slaves or war prisoners, and sometimes several hundred were killed in a single ceremony. The need for prisoners was one of the motives for almost constant warfare.

Aztec priests sacrificed people in the belief that the sun god fed on blood of human hearts.

Natural Dyes

The year is 1450, and your mother is teaching you and your brother the family trade of weaving. "Now that you have seen the pleasure of weaving a mat," she says, "we have to take a step back and learn to make the color for our fabric. We can use flower blossoms, berries, leaves, or bark. We also use the little **cochineal** beetle for red; it lives on certain cactus plants."

For your project in using natural dyes, you'll use wool, although the Aztecs may not have had wool until the Spanish brought sheep after 1520. (The people of the Inca Empire, who lived farther south in what is now Peru, had wool from llamas and alpacas; they may have traded wool with Aztec merchants.)

You'll use onion skins for color—only the dry outer leaves. Yellow onions create a color ranging from deep yellow to burnt orange. Red onions produce a reddish brown.

You will need:

- one skein of wool yarn, white or any light color
- four short pieces of string
- rubber gloves
- large (4-gallon) cooking pot, enamel or stainless steel; don't use aluminum or iron—they will alter the color. The kind of pot used for canning is perfect.
- tap water
- large wooden spoon or long piece of doweling
- 2 ounces of neutral laundry soap, such as Woolite or Ivory Flakes
- 3 ounces of alum (available at supermarkets)
- 1 ounce cream of tartar
- paper towels
- 6 to 8 cups yellow or red onion skins (dry outer skins only)
- colander or piece of cheesecloth
- adult helper

Hint: To keep the yarn from becoming tangled, keep it in the skein and loosely tie a piece of string around it in three or four places. It's also a good idea to wear rubber gloves.

1. Fill the large pot with warm tap water and stir in the soap flakes. Soak the yarn in the soapy water for 15 minutes, then wash the yarn by gently squeezing the suds through the yarn.

2. Pour out the soapy water, and fill the pot about halfway with lukewarm tap water. Stir in the alum and cream of tartar. This is called a mordant bath; it fixes the dye and keeps it from running.

3. Add the wet yarn to the mordant bath. With an adult's help or supervision, bring the pot to a simmer. Continue simmering for about 30 minutes. Use a wooden spoon to keep the yarn under water. Turn off the burner, and let the yarn cool in the pot for about 15 minutes.

4. When the yarn is cool, rinse it in lukewarm tap water. Squeeze the rinse water from the yarn gently—don't wring the yarn. Place the yarn on paper towels, and pour out the rinse water.

5. To make the dye bath, place the onion skins in a piece of cheesecloth and tie up the corners with string to make a bag. If you don't have cheesecloth, put the loose onion skins into the pot and use a strainer later.

6. Place the cheesecloth bag in the pot, and add enough water to cover it. With an adult's help, bring the pot to a simmer and cook for about 20 minutes. Add more water if necessary to keep the onion skins covered.

7. Turn off the burner. Remove the cheesecloth and throw it away (with the onion skins). If you didn't use cheesecloth, pour the dye bath through a strainer into a smaller pot, then pour the dye bath back into the large pot and throw away the onion skins in the strainer.

8. To dye the yarn, add enough cold water to the dye bath to fill the pot about 3/4 full. Again, with an adult's help, simmer the dye bath for 20 to 30 minutes, or until the yarn takes on a shade you like. (The color will be lighter when the yarn dries.) Turn off the burner, and let the yarn cool in the pot for at least 20 minutes more.

9. Rinse the yarn thoroughly in cool running water. When the water runs clear, the rinse is complete. Gently squeeze out the water, remove the string, and hang the yarn to dry (not in direct sunlight). Allow two or three days for complete drying.

You can use the yarn in the next project.

Ofrenda

The year is 2006, and you are vacationing with your family in Mexico. At a village marketplace, you stop to watch a woman making a picture using brightly colored yarn.

"This is an ancient art of my people," the woman explains. "My family has been making these pictures for five hundred years. We call them *ofrendas*, which means 'gifts' or 'offerings.'"

While your parents purchase one of the yarn pictures, you ask the craftworker how she makes the pictures.

"I cover a thin board with beeswax," she tells you. "The sun softens the wax, so that I can press the yarn into it."

For your yarn picture you'll use glue instead of wax. The finished picture makes a great wall hanging.

You will need:

- several sheets of newspaper
- poster board any color, or stiff cardboard
- ruler
- pencil

- scissors
- assorted pieces of yarn in bright colors, including the yarn you dyed
- white glue
- transparent tape or masking tape

---

1. Spread a few sheets of newspaper on your work surface, and place your project materials on it.

2. Measure a rectangle on the poster board or cardboard, 6 by 8 inches. Cut out the rectangle.

3. Draw the outline of your picture on the board. You can copy the picture shown here or draw your own picture of an animal, plant, or an abstract design. Keep the drawing simple.

4. Place a single strand of yarn on part of your outline. Lift up the yarn and make a thin line of glue where you are placing the strand. Gently press the yarn into the wet glue.

5. Continue gluing a single strand all the way around the outline. Change colors any time you wish, starting a new strand where the previous one ends.

6. Fill in the figure completely with strands of yarn, applying a little glue at a time. Work from the outside toward the center, keeping the strands as close together as possible so that there is almost no bare space showing. You can use little scraps of yarn to fill in any bare spots.

7. Fill in the background in the same way. Start by gluing a single strand all the way around the outside, then work inward toward your picture.

8. To hang your yarn picture, cut a 5-inch length of yarn. Center the strand and place it about one-quarter of the way from the top, then tape the ends to the back of the board. Slip the yarn over a picture hook or tack.

Tin Rooster

The year is 1525. An elderly man sits outside his daughter's house, a one-room adobe structure in a village near the ruins of Tenochtitlán. The Spanish destroyed the once-great city in 1520. The house of mud bricks has very simple furniture: woven mats for sitting and sleeping, low tables, and reed chests for storing clothes. The kitchen is in an inside courtyard, along with a small shrine to the gods. The bathroom is in a separate building and includes a steam bath.

The man's son-in-law was killed in 1519 fighting against the Spanish invaders, and the widow raises their son and daughter. The elderly man was a skilled worker in gold and jade, but these materials are no longer available. The Spanish load all precious metals and stones onto ships to send back to Spain. He now works with tin and sells his work to Spanish settlers.

You will need:

- disposable aluminum pie plate, 8 or 9 inches in diameter
- sheet of white paper
- pencil
- scissors
- sandpaper: medium or fine grit
- ballpoint pen
- Magic Markers: red, blue, yellow, green
- stapler

1. Cut away the sides of the pie plate. Save the sides to make wing pieces and a stand. If the cut edges feel sharp, round them a little with sandpaper. Do this with all the cut pieces.

2. Copy the rooster pattern onto a sheet of paper with a ballpoint pen. The drawing should be about 5 ½ to 6 inches high. Trace the pattern onto the flat, round pie plate circle. Press the pen lightly into the tin to create a design that looks etched-in for the details, including feathers and dots. The more detail you add, the better it will look.

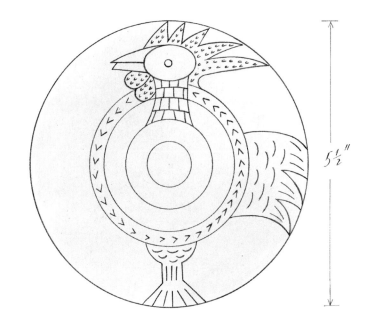

3. Cut out the head, body, and tail. Sand the edges.

4. Copy the wing pattern onto a sheet of paper with a ballpoint pen. The drawing should be about 2 inches wide and 1 inch high. Trace the pattern onto the sides of the pie plate, leaving 5 ½ inches for the stand. Cut out three wing pieces, and color all parts with Magic Markers. To apply the wings, start with the lower set, stapling it to the body on a slant, then overlap and staple the other two sets.

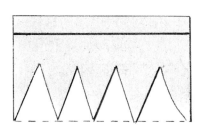

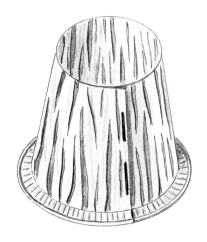

5. To make a stand, cut a 5-inch piece of the side. Overlap the ends and staple, as shown in the drawing. Staple the rooster to the stand. Bend the tail back a little for balance.

Glossary

chinampas: Very fertile gardens planted in a rectangular shape, made by piling up silt and debris from the bottom of shallow lakes.

cochineal: An insect that lives on certain cactus plants, used to make a bright red dye.

codex, codices (plural): An Aztec book, brightly painted and folded like an accordion.

conquistador: A Spanish explorer and soldier of the sixteenth century.

glyphs: The symbols in Aztec picture writing.

Huitzilopochtli: The Aztec god of war.

ideographs: Pictures that represent ideas or actions in Aztec picture writing.

obsidian: A dark natural glass formed by the cooling of molten lava.

ofrendas: A Spanish word meaning "gifts" or "offerings"; the name given to yarn pictures.

pictograms: Pictures or symbols representing objects or ideas.

Quetzalcoatl: The Aztec god of human life, often pictured as a feathered serpent.

telpuchcalli: Schools for young men that included military training.

tlacuilo: A scribe, or book artist; the word meant "one who puts down thoughts."

turquoise: Blue-green mineral often used in Aztec art.

Metric Conversion Chart

You can use the chart below to convert from U. S. measurements to the metric system.

Weight
1 ounce = 28 grams
½ pound (8 ounces) = 227 grams
1 pound = .45 kilogram
2.2 pounds = 1 kilogram

Liquid volume
1 teaspoon = 5 milliliters
1 tablespoon = 15 milliliters
1 fluid ounce = 30 milliliters
1 cup = 240 milliliters (.24 liter)
1 pint = 480 milliliters (.48 liter)
1 quart = .95 liter

Length
¼ inch = .6 centimeter
½ inch = 1.25 centimeters
1 inch = 2.5 centimeters

Temperature
100°F = 40°C
110°F = 45°C
350°F = 180°C
375°F = 190°C
400°F = 200°C
425°F = 220°C
450°F = 235°C

About the Author

David C. King is a freelance writer and historian who has written more than sixty books for children and young adults. While most of his books deal with American history, he also enjoys exploring life in other cultures, past and present. He and his wife, Sharon, live in the Berkshires, where New York, Massachusetts, and Connecticut come together. They have coauthored several award-winning books.

Find Out More

Books

Ardagh, Philip. *The Aztecs.* History Detectives series. New York: Peter Bedrick
    Books, 2000.

Baquedano, Elizabeth. *Aztec, Inca and Maya.* Eyewitness Books. New York:
    Dorling Kindersley Publishing, 2000.

McManus, Kay. *Land of the Five Son.* Looking at Aztec Myths and Legends series.
    Lincolnwood, IL: NTC Publishing Group, 1997.

Nicholson, Sue. *Aztecs and Incas: A Guide to the Precolonized Americas in 1504.*
    New York: Larousse Kingfisher Chambers, 2000.

Web Sites

Ancient Aztec Civilization
www.kidskonnect.com/AncientAztec/AncientAztecHome.html

Aztec Civilization
www.crystalinks.com/aztecs.html

Latin Art Mall: The Aztecs
www.latinartmall.com/Aztecs.htm

Index